Majin Magica

Part 1

By Lorenzo Wilson

Episode 1 Welcome To Oasis

Scene: It is early noon in the vast wide and barren deserts in the Southern district of Maven. The loud sound of the train echoes along the train tracks.

Trinity: * Sigh I wonder if the captain even put in at least a decent few words for us we really need this work. It would be a freaking shame if we came all the way from those slums of hell to get sent back. Hey, Rinne wake up Ennead we'll be stopping midway before we arrive. The captain said that we're gonna be meeting Amoria here.

Rinne: Really yay!!! I can't wait Ms. Amoria is always so good to us.

Trinity: I know she's been with us 3 years now. The best part is that she volunteered to be our escort with zero charges.

Rinne: yeah especially in these parts we are more vulnerable than ever.

Trinity: The captain said that those joining the guild have to be escorted properly to Oasis and that no one is really brave enough to do it unless they are heavily compensated. Oh look We've seemed to come to the midway stop. Get him up Rin.

Scene: Ennead is fast asleep on the warm lap of Rinne. She smiles and brushes back his bangs gently while rubbing through his hair.

Rinne: We're here wakey Ennead.

Scene: Ennead is still fast asleep Trinity looks over at him with a stern look as he's sleeping soundly. She begins to be slightly irritated. Trinity has a childlike attitude and gets impatient very quickly especially when things don't go her way or someone disobeys her orders. She gets up and wacks Ennead right on the nogging.

Ennead: ahhh!!! What what's going on?

Rinne: We're at the first stop before we make it to our new home!!

Ennead: oh really? That's fantastic!!

Trinity: pfft not like it's gonna do us any good at least for now that's if we make it there first.

Rinne: is it really true what they say about these parts? That no one really ever can fully make it to Oasis?

Trinity: There's no doubt about it the very fact that we are getting this ride has extreme risk levels. This area has been highly critical since the Venusian War.

Ennead: but that was nearly half a century ago. I think it's all just talk now since we've made it this far...

Scene: before Ennead could ever finish his full sentence the atmosphere of absolute silence and the eerie aura of death struck all three of them. The entire train was slaughtered mercilessly. Pools of blood entrails and ligaments spread across the deck of the train. Trinity responds almost immediately to the situation. She unsheaths two blue katanas and charges up her mana. Red streaks of electricity arc from her blades. She stands in front of both Rinne and Ennead as demons surround and board the train.

Rinne: Ennead stay close to me.

Ennead: oh-oh ok.

Scene: Ennead gives Rinne a talisman card with a seal on it. They both hold it to activate it with their mana. Out from the talisman comes a large sniper rifle.

Trinity: Rinne cover me!

Rinne: I'm on it!

Scene: as demons surround them Trinity starts slicing and dicing left and right. Rinne fires shots off killing demons in rows at a time aiming at their weak point. Ennead sticks next to Rinne ready to defend with his shield in his left hand. As Trinity is fending off most of the demons she gets cornered by 4 demons. One slides in from her left side knocking her off her feet. The other one picks her up and slings her through the train. One of the demons then punches her in the stomach she coughs up a bit of blood and gets elbowed in the back by another demon that knees her in the gut. As she stumbles she sees an opening and fires an electric blast from her katana from her right hand and obliterates both demons. 3 more demons show up to cut her off from getting back inside the train. Rinne shoots one but the other 2 charge Trinity. Ennead sees this and immediately rushes outside.

Rinne: Ennead!!! Wait!!!

Scene: Trinity coughs a little holding her side as the 2 demons are about to attack her.

Trinity: that idiot broke formation...

Scene: as everything unfolds a tall middle-aged woman with blue hair and

brown fair skin leaped in the air and dropped down right on top of one of the demons and blasted the next with a condensed air pressure stream of water as Ennead made it Trinity.

Demons begin to scatter at the sight of this unfolding.

Episode 2 Traveling

Amoria: ew.... talk about a mess. Damnit, wish I could have made it here sooner.

Trinity: idiot you broke formation

Ennead: stay still I've gotta heal ya up.

Rinne: Ms. Amori!!!

Scene: Rinne sees Amoria and runs over to her full of joy and excitement. Ennead continues to help Trinity to her feet. She only has a few scapes here and there. Ennead starts to charge his mana and a white tingling light envelope around Trinity. Amoria sees this and is especially surprised. The last she saw Ennead was 1 year ago and he wasn't even able to do what he's doing now.

Amoria: Say Ennead what is that I've never seen this form of healing magic before.

Scene: Trinity looks to the left and Rinne looks towards Trinity and Ennead.

Rinne: Ennead?

Ennead: well I um..

Trinity: He's a synergist.

Amoria: Hmm is that right.

Scene: Amoria is a bit surprised by this synergists are not well known and taken into account. Synergists are non-combating types that can link up their energies with others. Most synergists have an array of support moves and even healing types that shield their teammates and can do an area of effect damage. There are many types of Synergists though they are rare as of now due to being replaced by Saboteurs.

Saboteurs are more valued and wanted than synergists.

Amoria: that aside we all have to get outta here fast this isn't the last of them.

Trinity: You can't be serious?

Ennead: all those people on the train...

Trinity: there's nothing we can do even the military won't get involved in these parts it is all free gain.

Ennead: so we just leave and not try to call for any help?

Amoria: Ennead Trinity is right in these parts there's nothing we can do. There is no safe place or jurisdiction to pass these borders and for good reason, there's just not enough manpower and places to support these places. We have to make sure to take care of ourselves first remember. Now let us move quickly and get you all to Oasis.

Scene: Trinity Rinne Amoria and Ennead all sprint off in the direction of the train tracks. They have to make it out because more demons are bound to show up afterward. And sometimes the bigger nastier ones that even higher ranking officers have trouble with. Amoria is familiar with the area so it's easier to spot and see when monsters are approaching. As they are sprinting Trinity poses a question.

Trinity: Amori there hasn't been any contact with the captain for some time why is that? He knows we are coming right?

Amoria: to be fair he has no clue about you guys and you all even passed the training. I can't believe you three passed either. I expected you three would be shipped somewhere in a less harsh field, unlike this one. Especially you Ennead this is not for someone like you.

Rinne: what do you mean by that Ms. Amori?

Without Ennead, there is no way we could have

ever gotten this far. Trinity knows it too.

Scene: Trinity feels a bit of guilt thinking back

to the time when she was in training and

Ennead used a low-level talisman to guard her

against being double-teamed. She was so full of

herself during those times too but when it came

down to it in those moments she needed

Ennead's support no matter how many times

she tried to dismiss it. Rinne stands up for

Ennead the most. He is very important to her

she loves him so deeply and fully and

understands him. Rinne fell for Ennead when

they were really young at only 7 and 8 years old.

Ennead is the youngest of the three and has no

known parents just like Rinne they were both

orphans living in one of the most savage and

dangerous places known as LeBlanc. Not much

is known about Leblanc other than it was

originally a test facility gone completely wrong.

There were only certain safe zones which were

highly top secret and mostly no one really

dared much to go into Leblanc even before or

after it was shut down. The fact that Rinne and

Ennead survived in this area is astonishing as

only some of the most fearsome warriors could

manage to be there.

Episode 3 Demons Ghouls Monsters

Amoria: All alright ok I was just pulling ya chain there little Ms.

Scene: Amoria thinks to herself that Ennead is a lucky guy to already have someone like Rinne to be in love with him so much this early in life. Also, she realizes Trinity is also in love with Ennead despite her not showing it and pushing it to the side. Though Ennead takes more of a liking to Trinity because of this. Amoria is someone who can read people really well and she sees one hell of a love triangle.

Trinity: the captain doesn't know anything is what you're saying so how are we supposed to get into Oasis without him signing our contracts because we are already certified to be trained as full-blown assassins here.

Amoria: yeah about that I personally do not think becoming assassins is right for any of you. There's so much at stake and it's guaranteed death. I'm sure your captain knows better than to let you three get into Oasis.

Trinity: we know this already and still we all three have one goal in mind

Amoria: and what goal is this that's more important than your lives? You have plenty of options why settle for this!

Trinity: and that's the point we could all just settle in and do what is necessary but how is that right for us? Our goal is to end the disputes between the ruling empires!

Scene: Amoria hears this and begins to track back down to her memory of when she first became an official assassin. She was already an assassin at age 7 due to her race's genes developing faster than normal humans. She had one of the same dreams as Trinity when she was younger. This sparked a bit of hope and understanding of not only herself but the rest of the three as well. Amoria doesn't really approve of the three to become assassins but she realizes that maybe it's still possible to help and support them to make it happen. There's no stopping them at all.

Amoria: oh I understand no room for small talk so ok I'll help take you all straight to Oasis so that they can give you instructions on what's next. I'll even tell them that I'm interested in having you a part of my division instead of that captain of yours.

Scene: as Amoria tells them this they are a lot more cheerful and grateful to her. Their dream is to end the disputes between the ruling empires. Because of these disputes, many lives are lost and tragedy transpires from the most unlikely of places. Trinity Ennead and Rinne all share very similar beliefs and each has trained with each other daily. They know each other's strengths and weaknesses.

Amoria: we will be at Oasis shortly so hang in there yall.

Rinne: hey Ennead are you alright?

Trinity: he's slowing down due to mana deficiency we've got no choice but to find a resting area and quick!

Rinne: I'm running low on mana too

Trinity: sigh* same here

Amoria: oh ho ho so sorry I forgot you all are

still in training personnel even though you have

those cards that say otherwise.

Let's get to some cover first.

Scene: Right as Amoria said that she is pierced

in both legs with large spikes from a mid-range

distance. These spikes pin her to a nearby tree.

Demons show up and intercept them while they

try to go to Amoria.

Rinne: Ms. Amori!!!!

Trinity: can it Rinne get down!!

Scene: Trinity grabs Rinne in lighting speed

with her mana charge to help her avoid getting

hit with spikes and fire from a mid-range

distance.

Ennead: damn it!

Scene: Ennead gets cut off by 2 demons as he is trying to help Rinne and Trinity. They are all very low on mana and having encountered these monsters is a huge upset not only that but they are only a few blocks away from the Oasis headquarters. Trinity and Rinne are fighting really hard to maintain. Rinne pulls out one of the talisman cards Ennead gave to her. She activates it and 2 large greatswords appear with Ice swirling.

Trinity: Rinne that's the last of your mana you'll die!!!!

Episode 4 Come On Ennead

Scene: Right as Amoria said that she is pierced in both legs with large spikes from a mid-range

distance. These spikes pin her to a nearby tree.

Demons show up and intercept them while they try to go to Amoria.

Rinne: Ms. Amori!!!!

Trinity: can it Rinne get down!!

Scene: Trinity grabs Rinne in lighting speed with her mana charge to help her avoid getting hit with spikes and fire from a mid-range distance.

Ennead: damn!

Scene: Ennead gets cut off by 2 demons as he is trying to help Rinne and Trinity. They are all very low on mana and having encountered these monsters is a huge upset not only that but they are only a few blocks away from the Oasis headquarters. Trinity and Rinne are fighting really hard to maintain. Rinne pulls out one of the talisman cards Ennead gave to her. She activates it and 2 large greatswords appear with Ice swirling.

Trinity: Rinne that's the last of your mana you'll die!!!!

Rinne: No I'm not!

Scene: Rinne jumps in the air and travels in spinning motions making an ice pillar as she skates in the air and around the trees fighting multiple demons at once. There's no stopping her but she's exhausted to the point of no return and it's killing her while her manna depletes faster and faster. She's coughing up blood as she still slashes away. Rinne is giving it her all because she believes it will buy her time so she can't leave her friends behind and it's only a matter of time before she crumbles. But she is so determined that she unlocks another seal on her weapon and ice shoots everywhere into the air and doesn't stumble. Although she coughs up blood and is on the verge of death she manages to fight all of the demons off with this final attack. Trinity and Ennead are concerned and can't believe Rinne is capable of something like this. She had no chance and had used up all of her reserves. Amoria is astonished that

Rinne can even still stand.

Amoria: you? why you are unbelievable. There's

no way I'm letting you do that shit again you're

lucky to be alive and even standing.

Trinity: Rinne that was careless of you! Just how

much was that worth? Just what was that?!

Scene: Rinne thinks to herself that the reason is

that her love for Ennead is so strong that even if

she falters she will not give up a single inch

and make it stand with her own will because

she believes she can make it despite her

abilities. And she pushed far beyond her

thresholds and still was able to make it in the

end. Rinne is not as strong as Trinity but her will

and determination are unbreakable because

she has been through so much and can't

imagine losing Ennead or the rest.

Episode 5 Breaking Formation

Ennead: Rinne! Are you alright?

Rinne: yeah Ennead I'm alright......

Amoria: Trinity is right Rinne you used up all your mana we are getting you HQ ASAP. Ennead save your heals you we still have some time before we arrive.

Scene: Rinne lost for words and not feeling all pumped up like she was. She put her life and her comrade's life in danger for what she has done. She disobeyed Orders and took matters into her own hands.

Scene: Amoria Rinne Trinity and Ennead all gather up and make their way toward an elongated mountain pass filled with lush trees, they can hear the sound of rushing water. They see someone with mid-length reddish-brown hair. It's their old captain! He is talking with a much taller and elderly person.

Makios: There's not much we can do until we can find a way to rebound that place somewhere else, somehow. We can't have the Condourian knights crashing in on this mission.

Ivan: Well that won't be a problem now that I have finally paid off Eindra. And we now have an alliance with the Khalifaehs. It may be temporary due to trading routes but you understand there's nothing to be worried about

Leceiro will be there to keep watch so we've got it under control. There is a small banquet for the young prince before his official wedding so the Jhauropian empire will be on its best behavior that week.

Makios: Eh oh well... if you say so on the contrary I worry about that man The Venusian Empire will try something I'm sure of it and that's why I'm working on taking back something that they stole to try to settle the disputes that way. I'll be unguarded since

Leceiro has his hands tied.

Ivan: very well then it's all up to you we are

counting on your success.

Makios: you can count on it well I'll be on my

way.

Scene: Amoria Trinity Enneas and Rinne all

come up to Makios right as he's about to leave.

Amoria: oh well look who it is" Mr Reliable".

Scene: Makios looks and sees Amoria is cut up with several small puncture wounds here and there on her arms shoulders and thighs.

Makios: what the hell is going on with those injuries Amoria?

Amoria: oh that well yeah you see it. Too bad I'm alright you don't have to worry ok?

Makios: let's take you to the infirmary. Also Ennead you come with me as well. As for Trinity and Rinne, you both wait in the lobby until we can get everything situated. There's a lot we gotta discuss it's been a while I didn't think you'd all make it here at once.

Episode 6 Behind The Waterfall

Scene: Makios leads them to a small passageway where there are an odd amount of Palm trees and a giant mountain that looks to go on for miles. Trinity Rinne and Ennead are

troubled by seeing this. They need to get to a medical station and fast there's just no way they could handle traveling any further than they have. Amoria and Makios both look back at the three and smirk for a bit.

Trinity: hey what's so funny we are dying over here!

Scene: Makios turns his head and looks at Trinity seeing as she's all banged up with her clothes in tatters. then he proceeds to look at Ennead and Amoria looks at Ennead as well and sees that Ennead is holding up both Rinne and Trinity at the same time. Amoria gives Ennead a Mischievous look and smirks again this time with a sinister cackle along with an agreeable jester. Makios notices this and puts his right hand over his head as they continue to travel through the forest of palm trees. Ennead accidentally takes a look and sees both Trinity's and Rinne's breasts pressed up against his chest and shoulders. Ennead blushes and gives Makios and Amoria an irritated stare. Both Trinity and Rinne have no real clue as to what's going on other than they are Hungry stranded close to dehydration and exhausted.

Makios: Sheesh Yeah yeah I get it the Jig is up, look no further we are finally here.

Scene: Trinity Rinne and Ennead are confused as they see nothing but more trees and more desert along the way they are traveling. Makios pulls out a small double-edged dagger with blue and green seals on it encrypted with many different symbols. He then takes the blade and thrusts it into a small crevasse in an oddly shaped rock and the rock lights up glistening as it reveals a largely hidden waterfall. The trees and other trails disappear.

Trinity: So this was not only special Illusionary magic but there was also an advanced sealing technique in combination with Astral Magic as well.

Scene: Makios didn't expect Trinity to figure out how this technique worked so fast and accurately. This startles him due to only some of the elite in Oasis know about the sealing technique used to guard Oasis. For her to figure this out Makios starts to remember just how skilled Trinity was in the past. She was the top student in the academy where he was stationed for 7 years before he left back to Oasis.

Her knowledge of combat magic is way above the average. But to find that she also knows a bit about some advanced forms of sealing magic is somewhat of a surprise to him. Amoria is not as surprised as Makios is due to Amoria

is the one who taught Trinity about seals after

he left their hometown. As Trinity Rinne and

Ennead walk up to Amoria And Makios a large

gate opens behind the waterfall. Makios opens

up a scroll and another seal is released right as

they get behind the waterfall.

Episode 8 The Oasis Headquarters

As they entered the gate they finally made it inside the oasis building and headed through the lobby. They see lots of different sceneries and people. This is like a dream come true for them as they are finally going to be able to live with their dreams to make it in Oasis to be assassins to make a difference within the empire and world. It's hard enough as it is that they've gotten this far together with each other. This is a momentous reunion that has helped them to remember why they have pushed so hard for so long. Oasis is an assassination guild made to settle disputes within the region. They are not aligned with any other branches or factions. They are separate from any other division which means whoever hires them gets to take the scoop to the other. And on most occasions, Oasis assassins can be made to go against each other on critical terms. It's not good on terms with other agents or neighboring lands. Though for this instance it works out in the interest of Oasis as its own neutral facility. Oasis can and will support all of its agents to the highest quality though they haven't reached a critical standpoint yet in the empire to be as big a threat. They do have a solid footing when it comes to new agents and recruits. Their entire foundation is built upon mostly olden principles that are there to benefit the overall aspect of what it means and takes to be an assassin. And the skills one must learn and possess at their fingertips.

Many divisions within Oasis are for more than just assassinations. Others can be for quality or combatants. Mainly the direction of Oasis is to keep the balance between the nations and empires stable enough to keep war from happening.

The last great war was called the Venusian War.

It was a war that was the most devastating of

any wars recorded. And you can bet that the

majority of the United Allied Nations want to

keep this from ever happening again. The

Venusian war started due to the change in hand

of the grand priest who married into the empire.

This caused the enemy empire known as Helios

at the time to join the Venusian empire under

law and they were not accepting anything less

than having their empire name under anyone

else's. Galileo the high priest fought until his

dying breath to protect both empires.

And yet Helios fell completely. Only so few

survived and it was critical of them to set up

before it was too late they knew this entire time

there was no way they could address the

problems that they faced head-on all at once. It

was too much for them and they wouldn't stop

for no one as it became apparent that they

didn't really care to think about the

consequences that prevailed them.

And they were not too late. They stood up as more of a family during that moment than an empire. And they made it in the end with what they could and they pressed onwards with joy knowing they had rebuilt their empire that had once been under threats from Helios. It was pretty grim and they made it through.

The high priest was a huge loss but not entirely in vain and it meant that there was more room for improvement so that they could manage on their own and not have to worry about any more outside disputes. Or so they thought? The Venusian empire has stood for 3 centuries.

They were mainly considered to be peaceful as many trading facilities with neighboring counties also catered to Venusian technology and food. It makes you wonder if there were any other empires like Venusia before they rose. It wasn't their fault for the invaders and pirates that plagued the lands as they had their people travel. It's nothing short of the best that it can get.

Although there were reasonable choices and decisions made within the empire that kept them afloat such as their medicines and safe technological practices that helped them maintain balance with other nations that were doing the same at that time. It's no wonder they were always working towards new paths and gaining new moral standing amongst other nations' groups and divisions. Venusia was joyous and prosperous in those golden ages. They were going to manage the future of their empire so that they could live on. However, that didn't seem to be the case and some thieves stole or rewrote history as they saw fit and never looked back for it wasn't in the interest to try to keep rebuilding the principles of the old empire.

Though for 3 centuries they were successful and they made it through once again. War after the war caused so much pain stifling and grief among them. Even racist remarks bigotry territorial disputes and contemptuous notions began to flood their region.

This caused a huge decline in their ways of life and thus spread more time into the inflation of taxes and enslavement of those, not of the preferred races of the empire. These were the dark ages that no one transpires to remember but it's there and only to behold and uphold the old structures and foundational principles, not the ones of old.

For them they celebrate the Venusia highlight

month in July as a way to give thanks for the

freedom of slaves in their country because it

was never been done before and they knew it

was all for the great choices in their factor for

they had balances for what they were unshaken

by and the mistakes of the past. Venusia was

willing to do any means necessary to break free

of their old past to start a new one that was

brimming with light and not of darkness that

would succeed from the empire that could

outlive any Dynasty.

Scene: Makios and Amoria lead Trinity Rinne

and Ennead down 4 hallways and past the Head

director's room. As they are walking Makios

stops and looks at Amoria.

Makios: Say Amori could you drop those two off

at the infirmary first.

Scene: Amoria pauses and looks at the three

and looks carefully at Ennead with a bit of inner

heartfelt concern.

Amoria: oh that's right I nearly forgot.

Makios: Ennead is coming with us after we drop you two off its nothing to be wary of we just need someone with us from the scene to file the report of what happened. And before you ask Amoria is not able to file this report because she has to report to the Head Director personally. Alright, I'll see you kids off only for a brief moment.

Episode 9 The Rouge Corporal

Trinity: ah well whatever... Just meet us back at the Infirmary when you're done with Ennead Old Man.

Scene: Amoria Escorts Trinity and Rinne around a broad corner with an opening that has many bright designs, archaic decorations, and exotic plants.

Trinity: Rinne he's lying to us about something

Rinne: huh wha wha lying? The captain wouldn't lie about something important.

Trinity: I don't know, although he seemed to be telling the truth I can't put my finger on it but he's not being fully honest.

Rinne: Well you know he works for the top brass now so he can't tell us everything like he used to. We aren't kids ya know.

Trinity: ugh that's beside the point, Rinne.

Scene: Amoria interrupts.

Amoria: what are you two whispering so frantically about? Don't worry about Ennead he's gonna be fine. Makios will tell you about his condition in due time right now you two are gonna get some rest.

Rinne: And food too right?!!

Amoria: Absolutely! gonna feed ya til ya pop well.

Scene: Amoria takes a look and sees Rinne's breasts. She thinks to herself " As if, pfft this girl's tits are already popping they're nearly bigger than mine, wait" she takes a close look and begins to feel a slight faint of envy towards Rinne's breasts. Meanwhile, Ennead is taken to Makio's quarters and has the seal on the left side of his neck repressed by highly advanced sealing magic.

Makios: Oh boy how much have I missed doing this.

Scene: Ennead is unconscious while Makios is mending the seal on his neck. Makios put another seal on Ennead 3 years ago. This is an extremely dangerous seal that if left

unattended could cause Ennead to run rapidly

possibly causing a level 7 hazard or higher

which is highly classified and must be taken

with serious measures and precautions.

Makios And Amoria both keep this a secret,

even from Ennead himself. As Makios is taking a

break from mana exhaustion Amoria knocks on

his door and proceeds to enter his quarters.

Makios: So let me get this straight Rinne must

have exhausted all of her mana to near death

otherwise the seal wouldn't have come this close to breaking.

Amoria: Although I've never seen her do something like this in the past before I knew it she had already pushed the threshold right there. She completely exhausted her mana which causes Enneads Mana to destabilize and get absorbed because he's the host. I don't know about you but soon we are going to have to do something about these two kids.

Makios: Separating them is the worst-case scenario. They would both die, one cannot be apart from the other for too long.

Scene: Suddenly Makios thinks to himself for a moment he has a flashback to when he and his comrades were stuck behind 2 Shavicen Dragons and they had no way to escape from them. One of his comrades who was a saboteur had almost literally no mana left. But he was able to perform a huge enough explosion in quick succession against both dragons and help the rest of them escape. Makios can't really remember the name of the technique that activates the emergency use of mana. It can drain lifeforce energy which is extremely dangerous.

Makios: well look into all that later but anyhow so you know that there's been a breach in the Venusian history logs. For now, we can only assume it is a level 1 threat. The empire won't take kindly to it but I'm sure they have their ways to manage it for now. The only problem is the history log that was breached was the file

closest to the Venusian war log. And those are

class S files that mostly only the Channeler and

top instructors here at Oasis have access to.

And well you get the idea of what's next.

Amoria: yeah I do it's up to us senior veteran

Assassins to do the empire's dirty work to take

the fall if those files were breached and it's S

class which promotes it to a level 10 right off

the bat. Those standards drive me nuts ya know.

Makios: hey it's alright furthermore after talking with Ivan we have a plan in store for this as a safety net.

Scene: As Amoria and Makios are talking one of the corporals comes into the room to relay a message to Makios

Episode 10 Adision's Plan

Corporal Assassin Adision: You won't believe who we just brought into us today.

Scene: Corporal Adison uploads a hologram from his watch that shows the files of the person they captured.

Makios stands up and is in grave utter shock and disbelief. He's astonished to witness something of this level so soon. Upon seeing how Makios reacted Amoria gets up and sees it too and she begins to draw tears.

Makios: where is he!? is he in a cell do you know who we are dealing with!!?

Adision: easy there big Makios don't worry we've got him for real this time not even he can escape from what we've had to do to him. He's not in a cell just yet we have him being transferred to an operations room for check-ups. That being said if you want to see him he's right up ahead.

Amoria: tell me just how were you and your squad able to even manage catching or even capturing him for that matter.

Scene: Adison makes a stern yet troubled look as if he isn't sure or comfortable sharing this information. He knew that it wasn't going to be taken lightly at all.

Admission: it was just my squad but 6 others. They have all wiped out none of them stood even a chance. Kyrinneles is in critical condition and is already probably gonna charged as no-contest meaning she may never be able to fight again though she is awake and can talk. It's no wonder they say he's the master escape artist. No facility or branch has ever been able to keep him held captive. Until now. Though truthfully we don't know about that yet.

Amoria: Adision what did you all do to catch him.

Admission: We made the thing yeah that thing. It's called the Thordein Seal.

Scene: Amoria is astonished and in an outrage, she envelopes Adision in a bubble of water rising to his neck to where he can barely breathe.

Episode 11 The High-Ranking Prisoner

Amoria: How could you.... even for him. I should

execute you right now for this!

Scene: Ocainus steps into the room and advances towards Amoria.

Ocainus: Amoria Chan don't do this. He's from the same branch assassin just like you and me. Sacrifices have to be made.

Scene: Amoria sneers at the sight of Ocainus. She can't stand him of all people, To her, he's one of the worst.

Amoria: shut up blockhead!!

Scene: Benedictine steps into the room next confronting both Ocainus and Amoria.

Ocainus: what do you want Ben furthermore why are you even here?

Benedictine: I happened to walk by to see what was going on. Plus Ocainus just because we're assassins doesn't mean we sacrifice others not even for a mission. Amoria stands down. Don't you worry I'll handle this go to the medical station to see the prisoner? You don't have any time to waste.

Scene: Everyone stops once Benedictine makes his speech.

Amoria: I am so done I've got to get outta here. This is too much for me... Ugh!!!

Scene: Meanwhile in the medical station Ennead and Rinne are sitting on the sofa while Trinity is on the medical bed since she was the only one to suffer from most of the injuries. The medical station is an open medical area with different levels depending on injuries. They are in Medical Station C. There are many other patients in the room but nothing serious in

Medical Station C. They are waiting for three

high-level officials in white assassin coats

armor and gear to open the door and bring in

someone with long blonde hair and brown skin.

He is heavily chained down with seals

talismans alchemy circles and trinkets. He's

also blindfolded. As he comes in with the 3

Assassins the Professor speaks with them in a

special code. A black round chamber with many

seals and inscriptions appears in the very back

and they all proceed to take him there. As they

are Walking past Ennead, Trinity, and Rinne the

prisoner turns his head in the direction of

Ennead Trinity, and Rinne and gives a sinister

smile. He opens his mouth but the only one who

can see or hear what he says is Rinne. He says

S-Rank-Prisoner: "Who are you?"

Episode 12 Rinne's Unsuspecting Encounter

This startled Rinne to her very core. Because

his saying this indicates that she's hiding her

secret from everyone. The secret of her being

one of the daughters of the Emperor of the

Enemy nation known as The Felzeinius Empire.

She was sent to Leblanc when she was only 7

because she was a failure as a daughter and to

the Emperor and her secret mission was to

assassinate Nineikushin Ennead Shadohel.

Rinne goes into a trance that feels like hours

but it is only mere seconds.

Ennead: Dang I'd never imagine seeing

something like that.

Trinity: I overheard that he's the one guy they have had a warrant out for 13 years or something like that.

Ennead: 13 years!!! Then why put him here this place is too easy if he's like that.

Trinity: hmm you're right though they say he was a student here that went rogue. In which he has extremely valuable intel they can't let go. But even so, once they are done with him he's most likely going to face public execution for his crimes.

Scene: as Trinity is talking Makios walks into to an open Medical Room. He hands the Professor a few trinkets with seals on them. He then goes on about to the black chamber with the prisoner inside but sees his students Ennead Trinity and Rinne.

Makios: oh you guys!!

Scene: Trinity gives a look of unsatisfactory. She feels as if Makios is not giving them the attention they deserve. Trinity feels distant from Makios even though he's taken care of her since birth. He shows up very rarely and this is upsetting to Trinity. So she acts like she doesn't care for him sometimes when she really does.

Rinne: captain!!!

Ennead: captain!!!!

Scene: both Rinne and Ennead run up and hug Makios. Makios is happy and yet starts to get flustered a bit at seeing Rinne's boobs and them being pushed up against him. Trinity sees this and scoffs.

Makios: So I heard what happened I'm gravely sorry for not contacting Viceroy Ivan upon your arrival. I don't know what I would have done if you all lost your lives because of me. These parts are some of the worst and demons are always making a scene especially now that trade is leaving and entering some parts of this sector of Maven.

Trinity: I don't really care much to hear what you have to say but you already know that so I'm just gonna be straight with you. Ms. Amoria is the one who deserves recognition she is the

one who was there and has always been there

for us. That's why Amoria is going to be our new

and rightful captain.

Scene: Makios thinks to himself for a moment

realizing that Trinity is absolutely right. He

thinks that he should let them do it though he

feels responsible. As he thinks he hears a

commotion going on in the lobby about a

quarter in a half down the halls outside the

Medical station. Amoria is pissed at the

Professors from Medical Station A. Because of her outburst, Ivan comes in.

Ivan: Amoria Halide you are hereby suspended from captain personnel duties for 6 months. I cannot have you commanding any undergraduate squads in this condition especially after you've damaged property.

Amoria: oh well piss on a monkey's ass who cares all you guys ever do is make excuses for what happens anyways. Ugh!! Damn, those ingrates.

Scene: Amoria comes by to see the doors open to medical station C is open with 2 Professors talking.

She walks in and sees Ennead Makios, Trinity, and Rinne.

Makios: oh dear...

Ennead: Ms. Amori!!

Rinne: Ms. Amori!! You made it here too we were all so worried.

Amoria: it's okay trust me my wounds heal much faster than the average person. Also, I wanna say something, and you too Makios.

Makios: Um yeah about that it's going to have to wait I've got to get going I'm sorry for wasting your guy's time here. But from now on that will no longer be a problem. Amoria take good care of them for me please you're better off suited as their captain and you all have great chemistry already built. I'll be taking my leave now.

Scene: Makios leaves the room and as he's about to make it to the open corridors he sees Ivan. Meanwhile, Amoria is astonished and praises Rinne.

Amoria: so Rinne I've changed my mind, you were remarkably badass out there in the field. For a moment I didn't think it was looking pretty. Before I even came to pick you all up I had already used up three-fifths of my mana. The reason why you all made it up to this point was due to Maki on our way through the station had to confront 3 waves of demons to even get the

okay for there to be passage or passengers in

this area. I'm really upset that all of those

innocent lives were lost and taken right in front

of your eyes like that but seeing as how you

three handled it so well it's already safe to

assume that all three of you have passed the

psychiatric training at some point. This is

usually not a profession for you types though

there are students here similar to you all that

are really young.

Trinity: Amoria will you be our new captain? We need someone with your skills and experience if we are to survive here. All three of us have made agreements in advance and you heard what our old captain just said about you in the past.

Scene: Amoria gets a pressured look on her face that's filled with shame and disappointment. As she's about to say something to Trinity Ivan and Makios step in.

Makios: sigh*

Ivan: Amoria I'm here to inform you after this meeting, Amoria you are suspended from captain privileges but you will follow orders under Makios until further notice.

Character List For Majin Magic Part 1

Certainly, let's provide more specific details for

each character:

Corporal Assassin Adision:

- Name: Adision

- Gender: Male

- Race: Human

- Age: 32

- Height: 6'0"

- Skills: Proficient in stealth, close combat, and leadership. Skilled in the creation of the "Thordein Seal."

- Quirks: Has a habit of tapping his fingers when deep in thought.

- Backstory: Adision is a dedicated assassin who rose through the ranks due to his exceptional combat skills and innovative tactics. He is a seasoned operative with a history of successful missions.

Makios:

- Name: Makios

- Gender: Male

- Race: Human

- Age: 45

- Height: 6'2"

- Skills: A highly skilled assassin and leader, proficient in combat and strategy.

- Quirks: Known for his calm and composed demeanor even in high-stress situations.

- Backstory: Makios has been a mentor to many assassins and is well-respected for his expertise in the field. He has a history of

successful missions and is known for his

unwavering commitment to the cause.

Amoria:

- Name: Amoria

- Gender: Female

- Race: Human

- Age: 28

- Height: 5'8"

- Skills: Exceptional combat skills, mastery of

mana manipulation, and strong leadership

abilities.

- Quirks: Possesses the unique ability to heal

quickly from injuries.

- Backstory: Amoria is a highly skilled assassin

with a mysterious past. She's known for her

determination and her unwavering

commitment to her squad's safety.

Ocainus:

- Name: Ocainus

- Gender: Male

- Race: Half-Elf

- Age: 30

- Height: 6'1"

- Skills: Expert in reconnaissance and

infiltration, agile in combat.

- Quirks: Often uses humor to lighten tense

situations.

- Backstory: Ocainus is a fellow assassin and a peer of Amoria. He is known for his quick thinking and adaptability in the field.

Benedictine:

- Name: Benedictine

- Gender: Male

- Race: Kraiven

- Age: 50

- Height: 5'10"

- Skills: Skilled in alchemy and gadgetry, with

expertise in defensive strategies.

- Quirks: Prone to grumbling but deeply caring

about the well-being of others.

- Backstory: Benedictine is a senior figure

among the assassins and is responsible for

developing defensive tools and strategies to

protect the organization.

Ennead:

- Name: Ennead

- Gender: Male

- Race: Elven

- Age: 22

- Height: 6'0"

- Skills: Skilled in medical practices and

healing magic.

- Quirks: Calm and empathetic, always ready to

lend a helping hand.

- Backstory: Ennead serves as the medical

support for the squad and is dedicated to

caring for injured members.

Trinity:

- Name: Trinity

- Gender: Female

- Race: Half-Human,

- Age: 25

- Height: 5'10"

- Skills: Proficient in combat and magic, skilled in quick decision-making.

- Quirks: Occasionally distant from others, especially Makios.

- Backstory: Trinity has a complex relationship with Makios and is known for her ability to make split-second decisions in the heat of battle.

Rinne:

- Name: Rinne

- Gender: Female

- Race: Human

- Age: 20

- Height: 5'6"

- Skills: Skilled in stealth and subterfuge, with a

proficiency in espionage.

- Quirks: Keeps her true identity as a daughter

of the Emperor of the Felzeinius Empire a

closely guarded secret.

- Backstory: Rinne was sent to Leblanc on a secret mission to assassinate Nineikushin Ennead Shadohel. She failed as a daughter and is now on a different mission to prove her worth.

Ivan:

- Name: Ivan

- Gender: Male

- Race: Human

- Age: 40

- Height: 5'11"

- Skills: Strong leadership and decision-making abilities.

- Quirks: Takes his responsibilities very seriously and doesn't tolerate insubordination.

- Backstory: Ivan is a high-ranking official in the organization, responsible for making crucial decisions regarding the missions and the welfare of the assassins.